Second Position
for the Viola

by Cassia Harvey

CHP255

©2015 by C. Harvey Publications All Rights Reserved.
6403 N. 6th Street
Philadelphia, PA 19126
www.charveypublications.com

Second Position for the Viola

2

Purcell, arr. Harvey

Rigaudon

And on the C string:

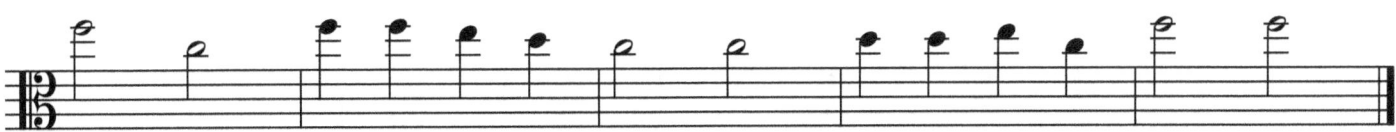

Breton Folk Tune — Stay in 2nd position. — Trad., arr. Harvey

German Dance — Trad., arr. Harvey

©2015 C. Harvey Publications All Rights Reserved.

3

Second Position for the Viola

A String

D String

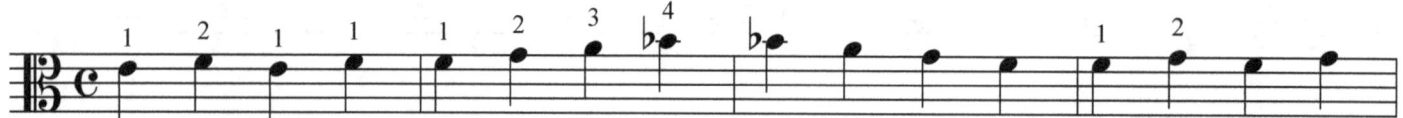

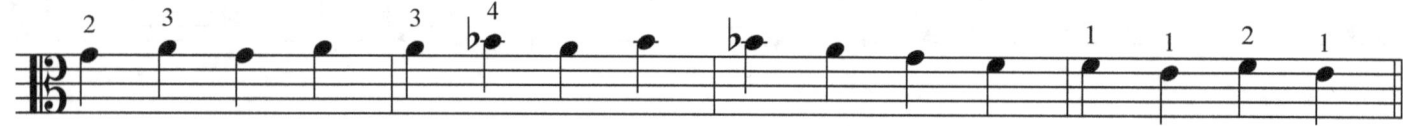

G String

C String

©2015 C. Harvey Publications All Rights Reserved.

Second Position for the Viola

4

Variations on a German Folk Song Harvey

Fiddlers Three Trad., arr. Harvey

©2015 C. Harvey Publications All Rights Reserved.

5

A String

D String

G String

C String

©2015 C. Harvey Publications All Rights Reserved.

Second Position for the Viola

6

Choral Fantasy — Beethoven, arr. Harvey

Aiken Drum — Trad., arr. Harvey

©2015 C. Harvey Publications All Rights Reserved.

7

Second Position for the Viola

Crossing Strings on A and D

Crossing Strings on G and C

©2015 C. Harvey Publications All Rights Reserved.

Second Position for the Viola

8

Tree in the Woods — Traditional, arr. Harvey

Folk Song — Trad., arr. Harvey

9

Second Position for the Viola

Crossing Strings on D and A

Crossing Strings on C and G

©2015 C. Harvey Publications All Rights Reserved.

Second Position for the Viola

10

Irish Fiddle Tune — Trad., arr. Harvey

Yosakoi — Trad., arr. Harvey

©2015 C. Harvey Publications All Rights Reserved.

11

Shifting on A

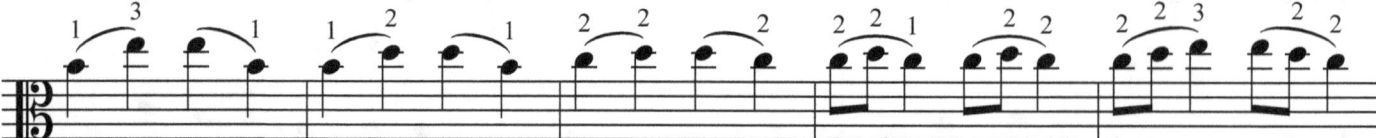

Shifting on D

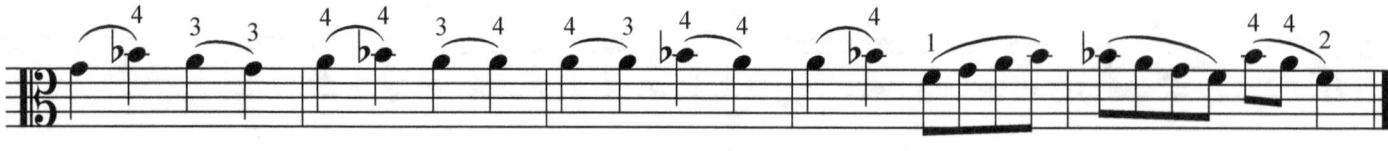

Second Position for the Viola

12

Shifting on G

Shifting on C

©2015 C. Harvey Publications All Rights Reserved.

13

Second Position for the Viola

A New Finger Position:
whole step, half step, whole step

A String

D String

G String

C String

©2015 C. Harvey Publications All Rights Reserved.

Second Position for the Viola

14

Dance   Praetorious, arr. Harvey

Russian Folk Song on D and G   Trad., arr. Harvey

©2015 C. Harvey Publications All Rights Reserved.

15

16

Second Position for the Viola

Contemplation — Harvey

Vivace — Harvey

St. Anthony's Chorale — Haydn, arr. Harvey

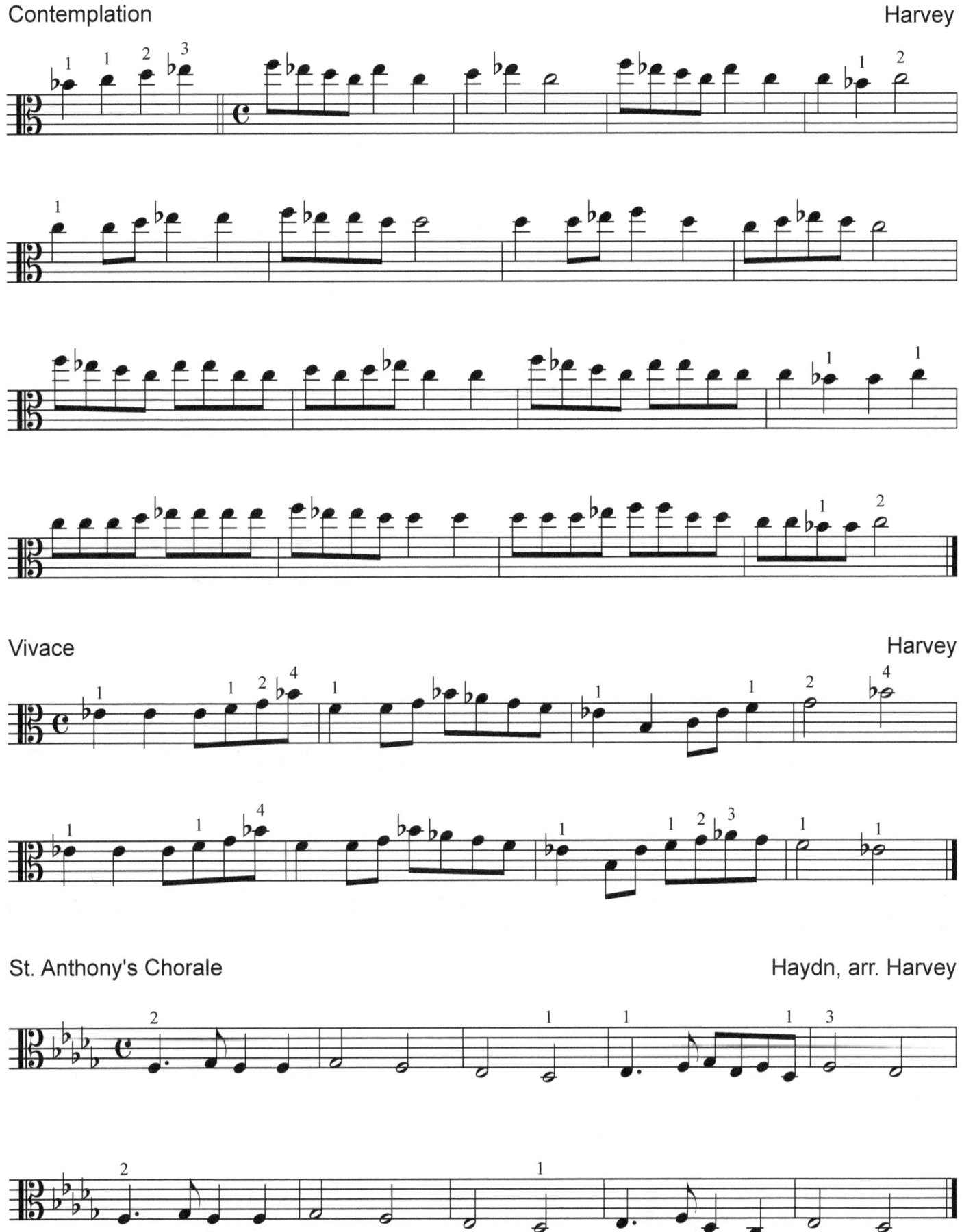

17

Second Position for the Viola

Skipping Notes on A and D

Skipping Notes on G and C

Second Position for the Viola

18

Allegretto

Campagnoli, arr. Harvey

Minuet No. 2 on G and C

Harvey

©2015 C. Harvey Publications All Rights Reserved.

19

Across Strings on A and D

Preparation for Country Gardens

20

Bohemian Folk Song — Trad., arr. Harvey

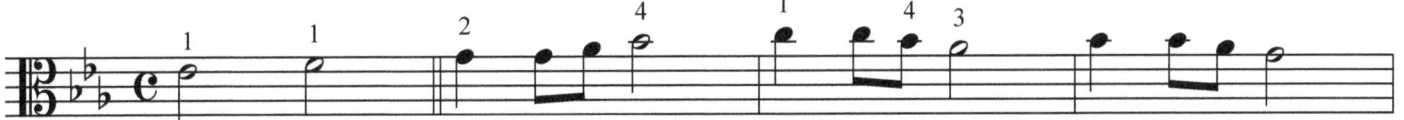
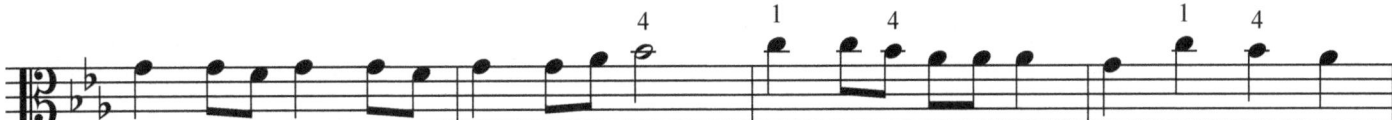

Country Gardens — Trad., arr. Harvey

21

Second Position for the Viola

Shifting on A

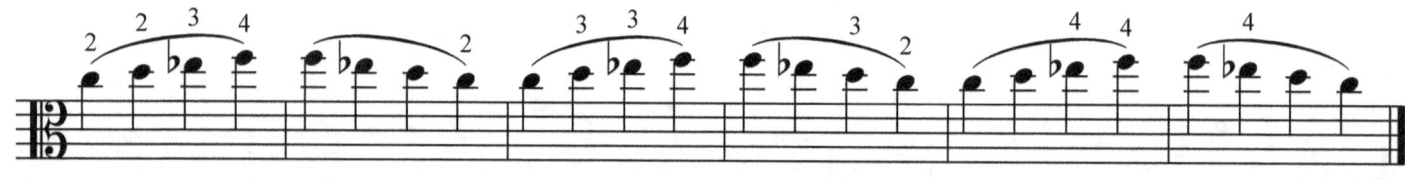

Shifting on D

©2015 C. Harvey Publications All Rights Reserved.

Second Position for the Viola

22

23

Second Position for the Viola

A New Finger Position:
whole step, whole step, whole step

Second Position for the Viola

24

Frenetic — Harvey

March — Harvey

25

Second Position for the Viola

Finger Exercise on A and D

Finger Exercise on G and C

©2015 C. Harvey Publications All Rights Reserved.

Second Position for the Viola

26

Allegro — Harvey

Peripatetic — Harvey

27

Second Position for the Viola

Crossing Strings

More Crossing Strings

Second Position for the Viola

28

Wandering Troubador — Harvey

Ukranian Folk Song — Trad., arr. Harvey

29

Second Position for the Viola

Shifting on A

Shifting on D

Second Position for the Viola

30

Shifting on G

Shifting on C

©2015 C. Harvey Publications All Rights Reserved.

31

Second Position for the Viola

A New Finger Position:
half step, whole step, whole step

Second Position for the Viola

32

L'Arlesienne Suite — Bizet, arr. Harvey

D.C. al Fine

Cadet Rousselle — Trad., arr. Harvey

©2015 C. Harvey Publications All Rights Reserved.

Second Position for the Viola

34

Rondo Allegro and Variation — Pleyel, arr. Harvey

Lady Frances Nevill's Delight — Anon., arr. Harvey

35

Second Position for the Viola

Crossing Strings

More Crossing Strings and Arpeggios

©2015 C. Harvey Publications All Rights Reserved.

Second Position for the Viola

36

My Heart Ever Faithful — Bach, arr. Harvey

Arlequin Marie sa Fille — Trad., arr. Harvey

©2015 C. Harvey Publications All Rights Reserved.

37

Shifting on A

Shifting on D

Shifting Across D and A

Second Position for the Viola

38

Shifting on G

Shifting on C

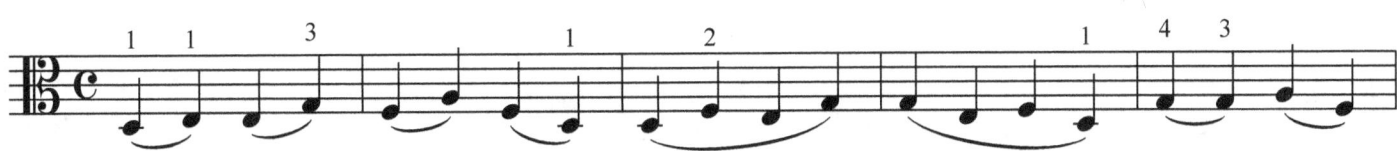

Shifting across C and G

©2015 C. Harvey Publications All Rights Reserved.

39

Second Position for the Viola

D Major Scale and Broken Thirds

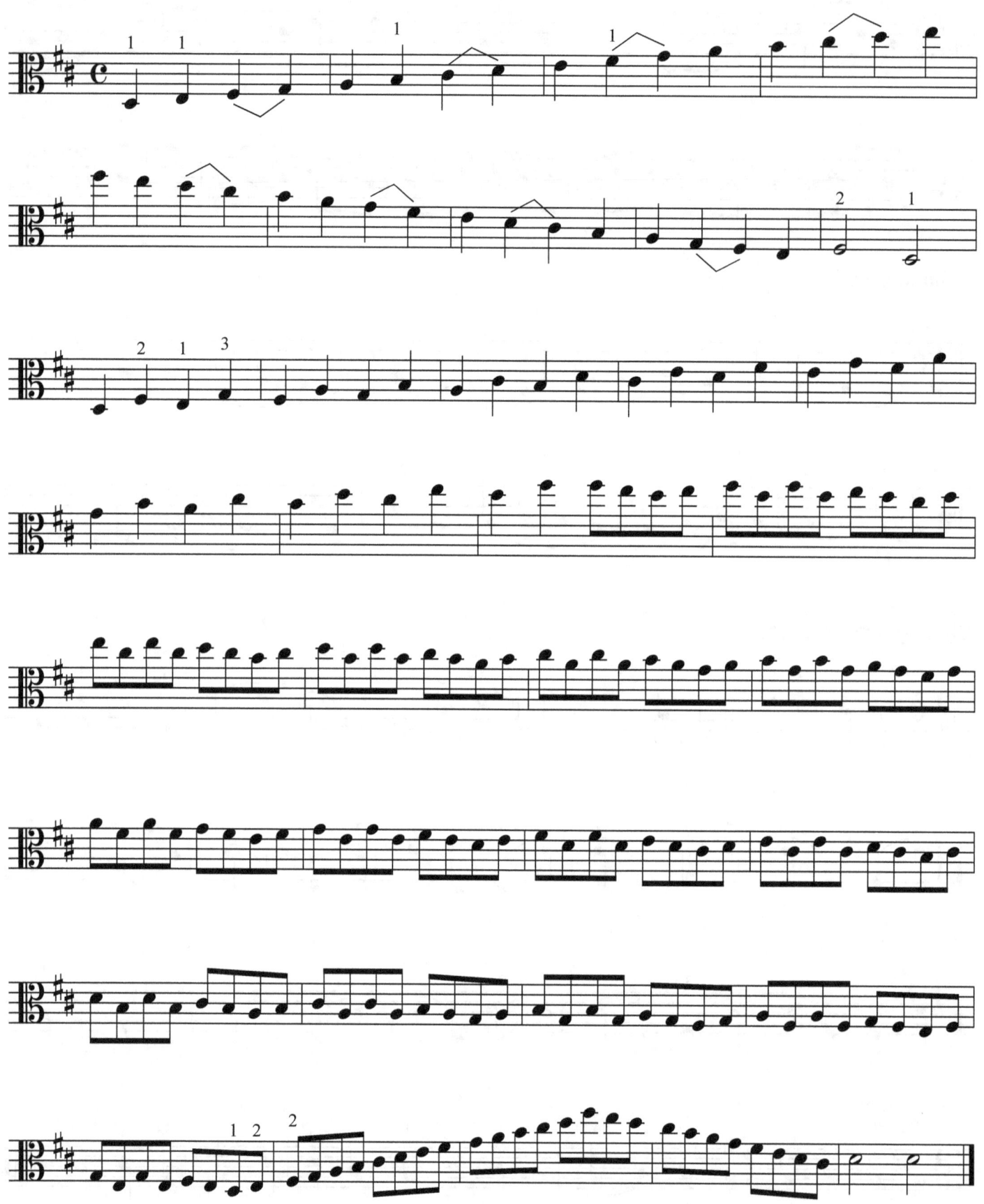

Second Position for the Viola

40

The Little Sparrow — Trad., arr. Harvey

Pray Goody — Trad., arr. Harvey

©2015 C. Harvey Publications All Rights Reserved.

41

Second Position in G Major

G Major Study

Second Position for the Viola

42

March Handel, arr. Harvey

43

Second Position for the Viola

G Major Scale and Broken Thirds

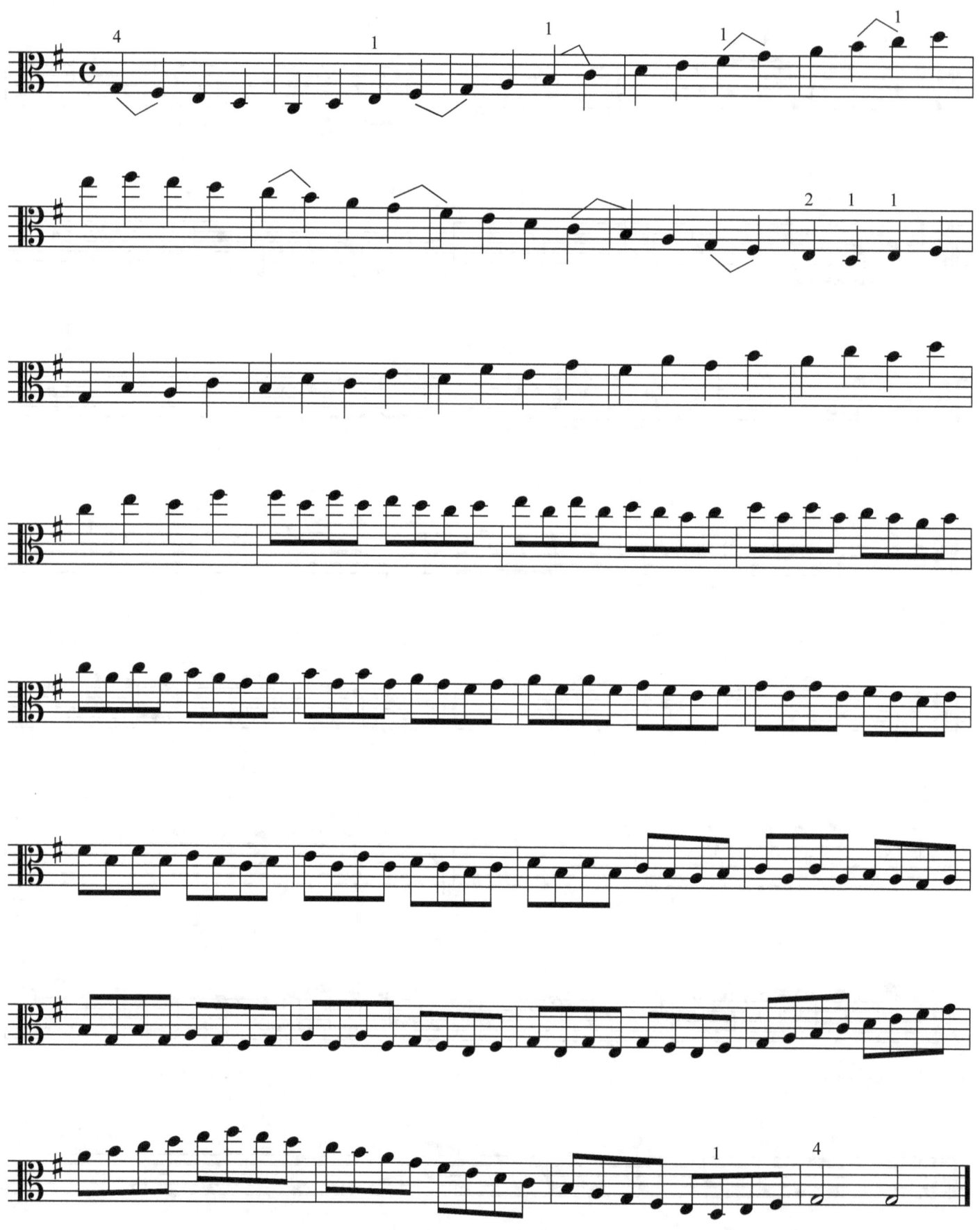

Second Position for the Viola

44

Polwart on the Green Trad., arr. Harvey

Jenny's Baby Trad., arr. Harvey

©2015 C. Harvey Publications All Rights Reserved.

45

Second Position in C Major

Second Position in C Major

Second Position for the Viola

46

Gavotte
Handel, arr. Harvey

The Yellow-Haired Laddie
Trad., arr. Harvey

©2015 C. Harvey Publications All Rights Reserved.

47

Second Position for the Viola

C Major Scale and Broken Thirds

Second Position for the Viola

48

Vivace
Raoul, arr. Harvey

Courante
Handel, arr. Harvey

49

Second Position in F Major

F Major Study

Second Position for the Viola

50

Poor Jack
Dibdin, arr. Harvey

51

F Major Scale and Broken Thirds

Second Position for the Viola

52

'Lavender's Blue' and Variations Trad., arr. Harvey

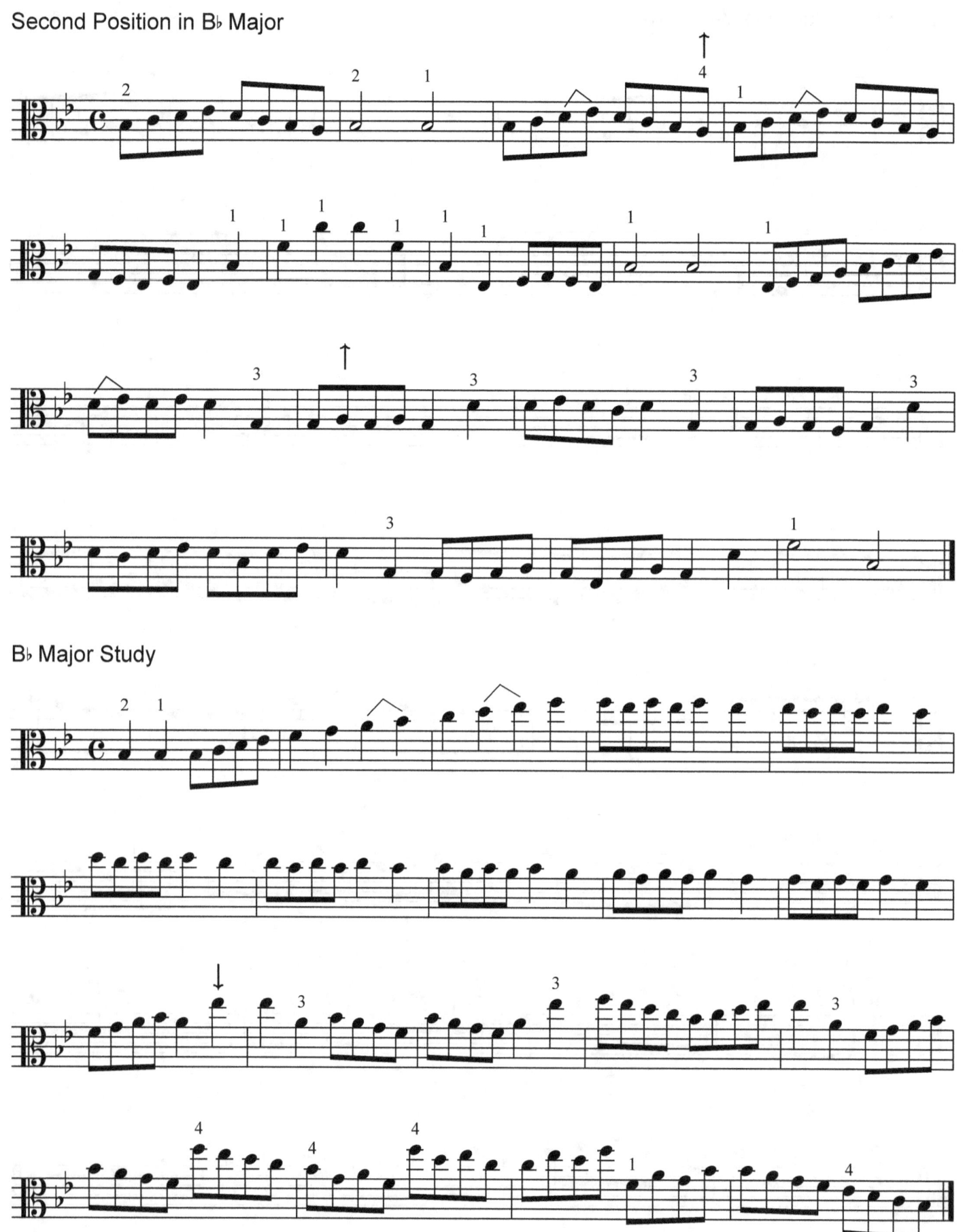

54

Second Position for the Viola

True Courage

Dibdin, arr. Harvey

55

Bb Major Scale and Broken Thirds

Second Position for the Viola

56

Slovenian Folk Song

Trad., arr. Harvey

Musette

Leclair, arr. Harvey

57

Second Position for the Viola

Second Position in E♭ Major

©2015 C. Harvey Publications All Rights Reserved.

Second Position for the Viola

58

Croatian Folk Song

Trad., arr. Harvey

Rigaudon

Rameau, arr. Harvey

©2015 C. Harvey Publications All Rights Reserved.

59

Second Position for the Viola

E♭ Major Scale and Broken Thirds

Second Position for the Viola

60

Ecossaise
Beethoven, arr. Harvey

©2015 C. Harvey Publications All Rights Reserved.

61

Allegro

Handel, arr. Harvey

Second Position for the Viola

Second Position for the Viola

E Major Scale

B Major Scale

F# Major Scale

D♭ Major Scale

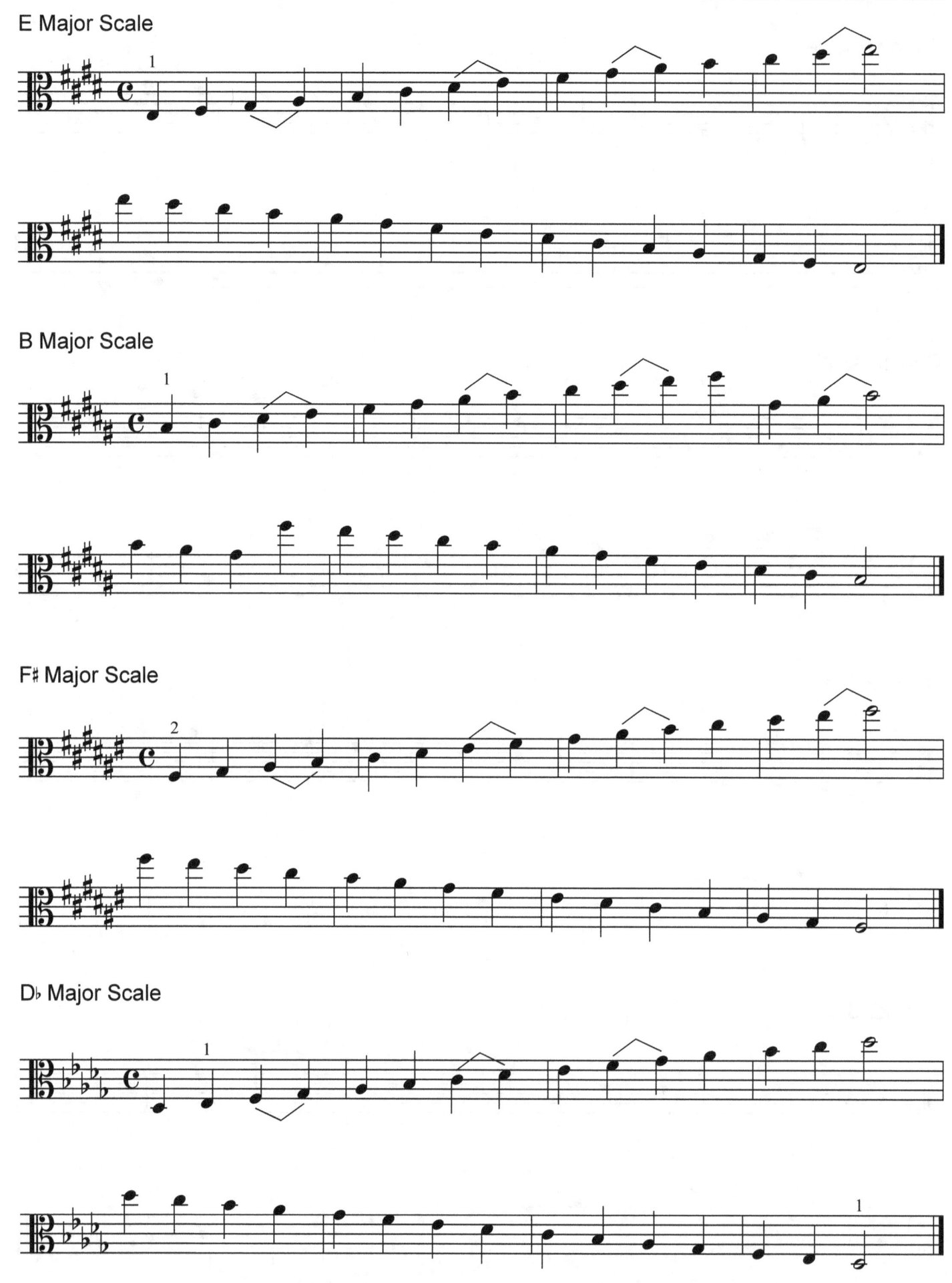

©2015 C. Harvey Publications All Rights Reserved.

Second Position for the Viola 65

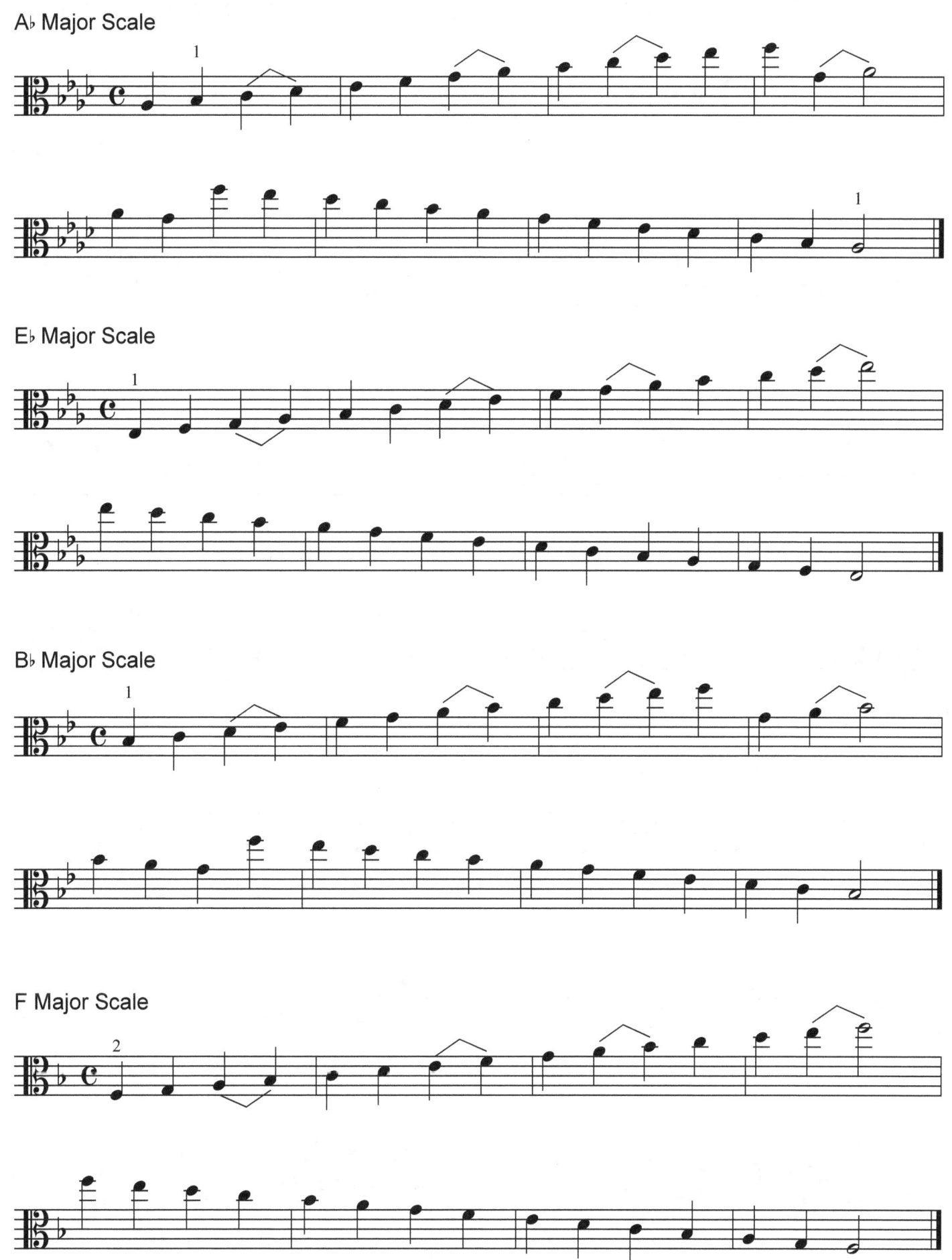

available from **www.charveypublications.com**: CHP258

C Major Shifting for the Viola
1
Cassia Harvey

©2014 C. Harvey Publications All Rights Reserved.